Radical Christianity

by
Norvel Hayes

HARRISON HOUSE
Tulsa, Oklahoma

Unless otherwise indicated,
all Scripture quotations are taken from
the *King James Version* of the Bible.

Radical Christianity
ISBN 0-89274-708-0
Copyright © 1982 by Norvel Hayes
P. O. Box 1379
Cleveland, Tennessee 37311
(Formerly *God's Boot Camp*, ISBN 0-89274-277-1)

Published by Harrison House, Inc.
P. O. Box 35035
Tulsa, Oklahoma 74153

INTRODUCTION

God, the Holy Spirit, gave the introduction to this book, when during the service in which this message was preached, the following prophecy came forth: Hear ye the Word of the Lord: Multitudes, multitudes in the valley of decision, for behold the day of the Lord is near. And when Jesus saw the multitudes, He was moved with compassion of them because they fainted and were scattered abroad as sheep having no shepherd.

He went up into a mountain and His disciples came unto Him and He opened His mouth and taught them saying, "Blessed are the poor in spirit: for theirs is the kingdom of heaven; Blessed are them that mourn: for they shall be comforted. Blessed are the meek: for they shall inherit the earth. Blessed are they which do hunger and thirst after righteousness: for they shall be

3

filled. Blessed are the merciful: for they shall obtain mercy. Blessed are the pure in heart: for they shall see God. Blessed are the peacemakers: for they shall be called the children of God" (Matt 5:3-9).

Therefore my beloved brethren, be ye strong in the Lord and in the power of His might. Shine as lights in a world holding forth the Word of Life.

GOD'S BOOT CAMP

Have you been through God's boot camp? Many people are right now in the valley of decision, trying to decide if they will be laborers for God. Whether you know it or not, when you got saved and the Spirit of God came upon you, you were drafted into God's army. You are now at the station, the church. The church is a soul-winning station. It is supposed to be a hospital and a place where people can come to get set free. If you are still at the station, you haven't been to boot camp yet. You've just been drafted!

You need to go through boot camp in certain areas of your life. You cannot do things for God that you haven't been trained to do. You can't do anything in this life unless you know how. There are people across this nation who are longing to do something for God, but they don't know how. You must be trained by the Holy Ghost.

A TRAINING PERIOD

Usually God will put you with someone or in a place where there are those who know God better than you do so they can train you. Just because you have the Holy Spirit in you and Jesus is your personal Savior does not necessarily mean that you know God very well. If you know Him, and He is in you through Jesus Christ, that will get you to heaven, but it may not help you to do His work here on earth. A lot of people have accepted Jesus and have been going to church a long time but have never really gotten to know Jesus very well. You cannot know Him any better until you have been to boot camp.

What is boot camp? Boot camp is a training camp where you get trained to be useful in God's army. Do you think it would do any good for God to send you to a place where you have to cast out devils and set people free if you didn't know how to cast out devils? NO! You have to be trained to do that! You have to know your authority as a believer.

Luke 9:1 says, *"Then he called his twelve disciples together, and gave them power and authority over all devils, and to cure diseases."* You have power and you have authority in Jesus' Name. When you have received the Baptism in the Holy Spirit, you have the power of the Holy Spirit inside of you to get the job done.

I John 4:4 says, *"Greater is he that is in you, than he that is in the world."* When you come upon a situation that you do not know how to handle, you need to remember that the One that is on the inside of you is greater than the one that has done the damage. But you can never be bold and speak with authority until you know who you are in God. You learn this from Jesus, but you must let God train you to follow His orders.

Luke 9:2 says, *"And he sent them to preach the kingdom of God, and to heal the sick."* The only way you will ever see sick people healed is when you learn how to let the power of God flow through you to touch and heal them. You learn this by going through God's boot camp.

One time a man from Canada came to stay with me for six weeks. He was saved and baptized in the Holy Spirit and he had come from a very social family. He had a wife and a teenage daughter and their community was about 98% Catholic. Nobody in his community knew anything about praying for the sick, casting out devils and setting people free. He was so hungry to learn but there was nobody there to teach him, and so he came to be with me for this period of time. He traveled with me and supported himself and wherever I would go he would travel with me and go to the services and just watch me. We would talk and share the things of God. He wanted to learn everything. This was his time in boot camp.

After the six weeks were over, he returned home, rented a high school auditorium and started a church. He began to preach the Word of God and to do all the things he had learned while he was with me. God moved mightily! He laid hands on the sick and they were healed. He cast out devils and set people free.

Now hundreds of people come to his meetings because his is the only Full Gospel work in that entire area — and he knows what he's doing because he has been to boot camp.

God wants you to go through His boot camp. He will put you where you can learn to be the kind of soldier He can train. Going through boot camp is not easy. Most people will never go through it. They won't pay the price. They won't allow themselves to be taken out of their comfortable intellectual, social or financial world. You must approach God with an open mind and spirit and ask God to mold you into the person He wants you to be and train you how to do what He says.

God woke me up one morning and said, "You tell the people that I have a job for every one of them to do if they will let Me mold them and train them. Tell them I have never made two faces alike; I have never made two mouths alike; I've never made two snowflakes alike; I have never made two sets of eyes alike; I have never made two personalities alike."

No one looks like you, no one says things the way that you do, and no one else can do the job that God created you to do! God never made two people the same, and He has a specific commission for you and your life if you will let Him train you in His boot camp.

HOW I WENT THROUGH BOOT CAMP

When the Spirit of the Lord first visited me, I was a member of the First Baptist church. I didn't know any one who really knew God and obeyed the Bible. I tried to avoid God's call on my life. I had so much pride that I didn't want to serve God with my whole life. I lived in a rich, social world. In fact, I even asked God to kill me instead of asking me to serve Him. That's how ignorant I was.

God wants to shake you wherever you are and jerk you out of your crowd. He wants to mold you and train you and God Himself, the Holy Spirit, puts you through His own boot camp. IT ISN'T EASY.

Have you ever heard of an American soldier who enjoyed going through boot camp training? No. It is not easy. It is hard. It is disciplined. You have to go through it and if you are not real nice about it you will get into trouble. In God's boot camp you will get into trouble with the Holy Spirit. You won't get any orders from Him if you won't obey Him. God won't trust you. If He can't trust you, if you are not willing to be trained, He won't tell you the things that you need to know to be trained. So you need to cooperate with the Holy Spirit. You have to be willing to do whatever God wants you to do.

You couldn't go through boot camp and still be in my First Baptist church. At least I

9

couldn't. Now you can learn to get people saved in a First Baptist church, but I wouldn't even let God teach me too much about that. I was in a real rich people's church with doctors and theologians, etc., and it was a very orderly and "dead" church! It stifled the Holy Ghost completely! At any rate, this is where I was when God visited me and began to move in my life. I didn't know what God's boot camp was, nor did I even want to go through it. If I had known, I probably would have run away.

THE FULL GOSPEL PEOPLE

As God began to deal with my life, first He moved me to Cleveland, Tennessee. In order to get me to believe the Bible, He sent a Full Gospel pastor to me. That was over 18 years ago. Now when a First Baptist man comes in contact with a Full Gospel pastor, it is a devastating experience! The first thing I noticed about him was that he would say things like, "Hallelujah!" right in broad daylight. It shattered me! I couldn't understand that. My Baptist pastor had never done anything as crazy as that. Then this same man would say, "Glooooooory!" The "glory" was so long and drawn out that it really made me nervous. Whenever he would say it, his jowls would shake and tremble and he would close his eyes very seriously. His by-word was always

"Hallelujah!" I really didn't know what to think of him, but I took a liking to him almost immediately.

God used that man mightily in my life to get me to obey the Bible. You don't obey the Bible unless you are trained. *"But natural man receiveth not the things of the Spirit of God: for they are foolishness unto him: neither can he know them, because they are spiritually discerned" (I Corinthians 2:14).* As long as you are living according to this natural world, in a world of man-made doctrines, you will never understand the things of God, the Bible, or the training of the Holy Spirit. You won't obey God either.

The next thing that happened to me was that this same pastor took me to a Full Gospel Businessmen's meeting. I walked in and another man walked up to me and introduced himself. I stretched forth my hand to shake hands with him and all of a sudden he grabbed my hand and threw his arms around me until he was completely wrapped around me and hugging me with a crushing bear-hug. Then when he finally let me loose, he slapped me on the back and just stood there grinning from ear to ear. I was embarrassed no end! To think that a grown man would have the nerve to hug another man, especially me, right in the lobby of the Holiday Inn. Of course the devil told me that everyone there was looking at me, but they weren't. The devil told me that and it made me all the more embarrassed, but you see I didn't know it was the devil! As I stood there trying to figure out why that man had hugged me, all of a sudden it happened again. Another man walked up to me, introduced himself and did the same thing! I stood there in a daze. Then I looked around and realized that everyone was hugging everyone.

The devil told me to get out of there and run for my life. He told me to run as fast as I could because all those people were crazy. In my mind I wanted to agree with the devil. But I stayed. One thing for sure was that these people were definitely different than any others I had ever met — ever!

Finally we went into the dining room and sat down. I was a nervous wreck by then. After we sat there a few minutes everyone began to sing. The very first song they sang began, "I don't care what church you belong to . . . ." That was enough! I couldn't believe my ears. Maybe they didn't care, but I sure did. After all, I was First Baptist and First Baptist care! I was really squirming by then. How I sat through that entire night I'll never know!

YOU MUST BELIEVE GOD

It is not enough to just love God and Jesus. Of course you are supposed to do that. It is the best thing in the world to know God and to love Him, but it isn't enough to help you. You must be willing to go into God's boot camp and let Him train you. Let God Himself do it for you. You must let the Holy Ghost, who is fire, burn the denominational doctrines out of you. Let Him burn out everything and every doctrine that is not Bible. I have learned from experience that Jesus can get the doctrine out of you. No matter what denomination you have been in, the Holy Ghost can completely burn out every doctrine that is not scriptural if you will let Him. When Jesus was talking with his disciples He said, *"Take heed and beware of the leaven of the Pharisees and of the Sadducees" (Matthew 16:6).* This leaven refers to the doctrines of men.

Now Jesus will be to you whatever you say He is. If you believe and say that He will save you and your children, He will. If you believe and say that He is your healer, He will be a healer to you. If you believe and say that He is a miracle worker, He will be your miracle maker when you need a miracle. You have to recognize Him as what He says He is in His Word and talk like He is what He says He is. You must do it without shame or embarrassment.

God will not perform miracles for you just because you need a miracle. Thousands of people have died waiting for their miracle that never came. You are responsible for what you get from God. You must rise up in your spirit and believe God for what you need. Jesus said,

13

"If thou canst believe, all things are possible to him that believeth" (Mark 9:23).

Let God put you through His boot camp. You will never recognize Jesus as your miracle worker, healer or deliverer until you go through God's boot camp.

Are you a person who is always wondering why God didn't do this or that? God will do whatever He says He will do in His Word. You must learn to believe Him scripturally. You cannot believe God your way unless it is in line with the Bible. You must believe God His way. You must go through God's boot camp to believe the Bible. If you go through your denomination training you will come out believing like they do. As long as you live like the world does you will never understand the Bible and you won't obey it. You will jump over the scriptures that challenge you and you will miss God's best for your life.

Check up on your teacher. The Bible says that the Holy Ghost will teach you (John 14:26). It is not good enough to say that your family knows God. That's not good enough! It won't get God to work for you, personally. Jesus wants to work for you and grant you your desires when you believe Him according to the Word of God. Any verse of scripture that you can believe God for, He will bring to pass!

THE BETTY BAXTER STORY

The testimony of Betty Baxter is a perfect illustration of God fulfilling His Word to one who will believe Him for it. Betty Baxter was born a twisted cripple. She had knots all over her body. She was fed intraveneously for fourteen years. All those years her mother said, "All things are possible to him that believeth. I believe that Jesus will come and make my daughter normal." She said that for fourteen years. She never wavered from her confession. She watched her cripple, deformed daughter grow without change for fourteen years and she would say, "The Bible says all things are possible to him that believeth." She hung a dress by her daughter's bedside and put a pair of shoes nearby. She would say, "Someday my little girl will wear her dress and shoes to church." But the girl was so deformed nobody ever believed her.

While the mother stood on God's Word, nobody else believed God with her. The husband didn't. The pastor didn't. Her friends didn't. Nobody did.

Everyday for fourteen years she reminded Jesus of that scripture. She would say, "I believe for You to come, Jesus, and make my daughter normal." One Sunday afternoon at three o'clock, the wind began to blow around the house and the curtains began to rustle in the breeze but the sun was out and everything was calm and quiet outside. All of a sudden a white cloud appeared in the living room and it got bigger and bigger. Soon it was real big. Then instantly in the middle of that white cloud Jesus appeared. He stepped out of the white cloud on to the floor and walked over within two steps of the wheelchair and looked at that little crippled girl. She reached out to touch Him but she couldn't reach Him. The mother said, "Jesus, if you will step a little bit closer she can touch you." He wouldn't move. He stood still. The little girl kept reaching to touch Him but she couldn't. She strained with all her might to touch Him but she couldn't. She reached so long, she finally fell onto the floor exhausted. She was a twisted, pitiful heap.

Then Jesus said, "I just wanted you to know that all of your effort without Me can get you nothing." Then He took one step closer and touched her. Instantly the knots on her body dissolved. The bones cracked and her limbs straightened. Her body was completely made whole in a moment of time. She jumped out of the wheelchair and ran.

Nobody had believed God to heal that little girl except her mother.

That night that little girl, Betty Baxter, stood in her church wearing that new dress and shoes. She had never worn a dress before, nor shoes because her body had been so twisted and deformed. Nobody preached that night. The news spread rapidly and people came from miles around to see God's miracle. Many people got saved, healed and delivered that night. The power of God was present in a mighty way. Today, Betty Baxter ministers to others. Doctors bring their impossible cases to her and God heals them. Her testimony is, "Nothing is impossible to him that believeth."

HUNGRY FOR A MIRACLE

Let me continue my story of how God trained me in His boot camp. It was through the Full Gospel Businessmen's Fellowship that I received the baptism in the Holy Spirit. Immediately I was hungry to see a miracle. I was willing to go anywhere any time to see a miracle. I had received power from on high to believe the Bible, but I hadn't seen anything yet. I had read the Bible and read about the miracles of God and yet I hadn't seen anything like these mighty works of God taking place in our day. I read in the Gospels where 5,000 people climbed up a mountain just to see Jesus and now I was just as hungry.

PRAYING FOR THE SICK

One night a friend of mine, a pastor, invited me to his church. After the service he asked me to help pray for the sick. As I prayed that night, my hands began to feel strange, as if the bones would pop right through my flesh. My Baptist hands had never felt like that before. I asked my friend what was happening to me. He told me that I was experiencing God's healing power flowing through my hands. I walked over to those sick people at the altar and began to lay my hands on them. One by one they fell under the power of God. It was all so new to me, but I knew it was God and it was wonderful!

Shortly thereafter God taught me how to be a channel for His healing power. I was at my house one day and my friend, a Full Gospel pastor, showed up. He said, "Brother Norvel, God told me to come and get you to go with me to pray for a Methodist woman. She is in bed and can't get up."

I asked, "Why can't you just go pray for her?"

He said, "I don't know. The Lord told me to come and get you."

So I agreed to meet him thirty minutes later at the church. We met there, along with the song leader, and we drove out to her house. We decided that since the woman was all alone we would stop and get her some food. She was just a young woman about thirty years old with three small children, and her husband was out of town on business.

When we arrived, the pastor spoke up and said, "God told me to bring Brother Hayes and pray for you." He told the song leader to stand by the foot of the bed, he knelt by the side of the bed and he told me to lay my hands on her and pray for her.

I touched her forehead lightly with my fingertips and said, "Satan, I take authority over you in Jesus' name and I command you to take your hands off of her. Now Lord, I thank you for healing her."

At that moment my right hand and arm felt warm. The power of God surged through my right arm and into her. Although I only touched her lightly with my fingertips, her whole body began to quiver. At first I thought maybe she was chilling or something. Then she began to shake. She shook so much that the whole bed vibrated with God's power. My right arm was so hot and I said, "Lady, the Lord Jesus Christ is healing you!"

She sat up and exclaimed, "I have never felt so good in my life."

I stood there with the ends of my fingers still on her forehead and she was still literally shaking. In a matter of five minutes she was completely restored to normal and all signs of illness had completely disappeared. She just sat there rejoicing and praising God. Tears ran down her face as she basked in the presence of Jesus.

As we started out of the bedroom, I turned to her and said, "Well people are supposed to be up and out of bed. Get up."

She got up and still rejoicing and singing

unto the Lord, she began to do the chores which had been left undone for several days. She was singing and rejoicing so much we couldn't even talk to her so we said "good bye" and left her singing and healed. A few nights later she came to a Full Gospel Businessmen's Fellowship meeting and gave a glorious testimony of how Jesus had healed her.

That was the way Jesus trained me to pray for the sick. Mark 16:18 says, *"They shall lay hands on the sick, and they shall recover."* You have to go where there are sick people in order to lay hands on them and see them healed by the power of God. Jesus said, *"I was sick, and ye visited me" (Matthew 25:36).* When? *"Inasmuch as you have done it unto one of the least of these my brethren, ye have done it unto me" (Matthew 25:40).* As you visit sick people and bring healing to them, so you visit Jesus. As you try to help people who are sick and brokenhearted and beaten down by life itself, you do it as unto Jesus. This is how you are trained when you are in God's boot camp. Until you are willing to go through God's boot camp you will never be able to appropriate the promises of God in your own life, nor will you be able to help others effectively.

SEARCHING FOR A MIRACLE

Meanwhile, my search for a great miracle of God continued. Several months later I heard about a meeting where a man named Lester Sumrall was going to be holding a revival. I had never heard of him, but I had heard that he was a man who prayed for hours before his meetings and that God wrought many miracles by him. I heard that a man attended one of his services who had infected hands and whose arm was withered. He previously had all the tendons taken out because of the infection. Before Mr. Sumrall ever preached a word, he stood up and said, "Will the man with a withered hand stand up?" Then he told him to stretch out his hand and he shouted, "In Jesus' name, hand, be made whole!" God's power went into that hand and God put new tendons in it. The whole church went wild with joy and amazement.

I was so hungry to see a miracle like that, I immediately began to look for Lester Sumrall. Within just a few weeks God had shown me such favor that Lester Sumrall had scheduled a meeting in our town and was going to hold a meeting in the church of a friend of mine. We planned the meetings with great anticipation. When he came he prayed for everything that didn't move! He cast out devils and prayed for everyone. We became friends instantly. After the meetings he would come to my home to eat and one night he invited me to join him in California for one of his crusades. He asked me to give a brief testimony of what God had done in my life. I was now proceeding along the path of God's boot camp. God had put me with someone to train with!

TRAINING ME TO CAST OUT DEVILS

Soon I found myself in the meeting in San Bernadino, California with Lester Sumrall. He asked me to give a short testimony of the work that God had done in my life. So, I did. That was the first night. But at that time the Lord impressed me to stay for the rest of the meetings and so I stayed for several days. After the last meeting, a woman walked up to me and said, "I believe you are a man of God. Every time I come downtown, pain comes on me and I have to call someone to come and get me and take me home."

I told her I would pray for her. As soon as my hands touched her, she jumped and recoiled from me. She clenched her fists violently at me. She growled like a mad animal. It stunned me completely. I had never seen anyone act like that before, especially in a church service. I didn't know what to do! I thought to myself, "Surely she won't try to fight me in front of all these people." But she just stood there growling at me with her fists still clenched.

Demons are bold and stubborn. They want to destroy people and do them harm. They don't want to leave.

While I stood there, everyone began to stare at me. What could I do? I thought maybe it would all go away but it got worse. That girl got meaner. I thought then that if God would just let me out of that situation, I would never bother these people again! But you see, God had brought me to this place in my training and I was right where He wanted me. But I didn't know how to handle this situation because I had never been taught. Even when I tried to ignore the situation, it didn't help at all.

There are many things that go on in the spirit world and you must be trained so that you will know how to deal with them.

As I stood there in front of this girl, all of a sudden she started to lunge at me. I held her back. Then, behind me I heard Lester Sumrall shout, "Cast that thing out of her." I looked at him. I looked back at her. She began to whine like a puppy and fell on the floor on her back, just whimpering pitifully. All this was new and strange to me! There I was in the middle of the battle with no training. What a mess! I didn't know what was in her much less how to cast anything out! Then Lester added, "And don't let her talk either." I just muttered, "Sure." I was so confused.

Thank God, another minister was nearby. He got up out of his seat and knelt down beside

23

the girl. He commanded, "In Jesus' name come out of her." I didn't want the people watching to think that I was a dummy, so I said, "Yeah." Then he repeated, "In Jesus' name I said come out of her." Then I decided to mimic him, but I really didn't have any idea what I was doing and I am sure I looked ridiculous.

God was training me, but I couldn't rely on another man's training. I had to be trained myself. That minister stayed by that girl and ministered to her until she was completely set free, saved, and filled with the Holy Ghost. After a short time, she yielded to the power of God. The minister said, "Thank you, Jesus." So I said, "Thank you, Jesus." Even then I really didn't know what I was saying, "Thank you, Jesus." That girl was laying there so still I thought possibly she was dead. All I wanted to do was get out of there. When you come face to face with the devil and you haven't been through God's boot camp to be trained, you are in real trouble! Soon, however, that girl started to cry and weep and get blessed and I began to realize that the blessing and glory of the Lord was on her. She got up – completely changed by the power of God and radiant all over. I had never seen anything so beautiful in my life.

After I returned to my hotel that evening, I cried out to God saying, "Is it possible that I have been so ignorant?" I had been so ignorant of the things that God wants to do for people.

He wants to set them free, to heal and completely deliver every person, giving them the glorious liberty that is in Jesus. It made me begin to seek God more diligently than ever. I completely submitted myself even more to the training of the Holy Spirit. I had so much to learn. But that night God had trained me how to cast out devils. Now I would be responsible to act on the knowledge He had given me.

It was right at this time in my life that God told me to begin to study Mark, chapter 16. I was being trained in God's boot camp. You need to listen to the Gospel, the entire spectrum of God's Word, or you will never do what God wants you to do. You will live and die and never see God manifest Himself.

The very next week after I had this experience in California, I encountered a girl who was completely demon possessed. But now I was equipped with Mark, chapter 16 and trained to obey God. I approached this girl and said, "In Jesus' name, I command you Satan, to come out of her." She fell to the floor. She was completely delivered, saved and filled with the Holy Ghost. The first time I ever addressed a demon, it had to obey. The Lord told me right then, "Never stop casting out devils. Never."

YOU MUST BE EQUIPPED

God will not send you to a place when you

are not equipped to do the job for Him. If you are asking God why He doesn't use you more, ask yourself, "Am I equipped?" Have you been trained? What do you know how to do for God? Have you been through God's boot camp? You will never learn how to pray for the sick until you go with someone and watch them pray for sick people, and then come to a place where you can believe it and do it yourself. Then you will be able to put your hands on sick people and see them healed. That is the way Jesus trains you to pray for the sick. You either know what you are doing or you don't. It doesn't take very long to learn, but you have to submit yourself to the training.

Have you ever prayed for a sick person and actually seen them get healed?

Have you ever used the name of Jesus to cast out devils?

God wants to train you to do the Gospel!

Many of you reading this book are in the valley of decision. Jesus wants to take you and set you on a mountain and teach you the power of the real and true Gospel and let you go forth in His name to this world. Are you willing? If you are not willing to go through God's boot camp, God cannot help you. If you are willing, God will train you. You have to come to a place to know that in Christ Jesus there is no defeat. You must learn to use God's Word and to mean what you say.

Many of you are now in the valley of

decision. You need to decide if you will enlist in God's army and go to His boot camp. The decision is yours.

I remember one night after praying for a demon-possessed girl who had been set free, Lester Sumrall and I were at our hotel. He turned to me and said quietly, "I guess you know that God will hold you and me responsible for teaching others." That is the reason for writing this book. I want to stir your heart by the Holy Ghost to have you boldly commit yourself to be willing to be trained in God's boot camp.

Maybe some of you once started and it became too hard. It isn't easy, but God will see you through. You need it. You cannot serve God effectively without it. But you see, I had to be willing to be trained. God will not take you and train you unless you are willing. I had to get with another man who knew God better than I did and study his ministry. I had to get into the Bible and learn who I was in Christ Jesus and the authority I had in God's Word. I had to be trained and go through God's boot camp in order to get to a place where I could really help people. I had to come to realize that I had the Greater One dwelling in me.

Now God sends people to me for help. I can't just pat them on the back and tell them to go merrily on their way and maybe someday God will help them. Unless the power of God can be imparted to them, they will remain helpless. God wants you to help others and if you won't submit yourself to His training, God won't use you.

You may be the person who wants to go through God's boot camp. Right now you are in the valley of decision. You don't know what to do for people who need help and you haven't made any effort to learn. You have to get hungry to do the work of the Lord. You have to have a real hunger that will motivate you to get into the Word and allow the Holy Ghost to teach you. You have to put forth an effort to get this training.

YOU HAVE POWER AND AUTHORITY

"Then he (Jesus) called his twelve disciples together, and gave them power and authority over all devils, and to cure diseases. And he sent them to preach the kingdom of God, and to heal the sick" (Luke 9:1 & 2).

This is the power and authority that God has given you to equip you for His work. You have power and authority over all devils and to cure diseases. If God is talking to you now and you have been in the valley of decision and you haven't been through God's boot camp, you need to make the effort NOW. Get before God and dedicate yourself to His training. Let the Holy Ghost teach you how to use the Word of God. It does not fall on you like the

28

rain. You must move in to God and be willing to go through His boot camp. You must be willing to lay aside your education, your social status, your financial situation. It is not easy. Many, many, many, many, many times it is embarrassing to some people. It shouldn't be. It seems embarrassing because many people are not used to being a doer of the Word. There are not many people who are really willing to minister to the unlovely.

It is a wonderful thing to be humble and to love Jesus. But you need even more from God. You need your spirit to be bold before God. You need to be bold in front of your friends. Take your stand like a soldier!

As you turn to God, He will do a work in your heart to bring you out of the valley of decision and set you on top of a mountain. He will put you in a place and with people who know more about God than you do and who are able to train you. He will cause you to hunger after the Word of God as never before and He will reveal the truths therein unto your heart.

MAKE THIS CONFESSION OF FAITH TODAY

I open my heart to you, Jesus. I ask you to come and do a work in me. Put me through God's boot camp regardless of the cost. Burn out the pride and embarrassment in me. I do not want to be ashamed of God. Satan has no authority over me. Satan, I command you in

Jesus' name to take your hands off of my mind. Go from me in Jesus' name. Jesus, I am willing to be trained. I am willing to go through God's boot camp. I want to see people healed and set free by the authority in me as I speak in the name of Jesus and I believe in my heart that He will perform His works through me.

I claim that I will be made a warrior for God. I will go forth with Holy boldness to obey the Gospel. I will not play games or play church. I will work for God.

God, change me into another person so that your Spirit can go forth from me to a world of darkness and set the captives free!

Books by Norvel Hayes

How To Live and Not Die

The Winds of God Bring Revival

God's Power Through the Laying on of Hands

The Blessing of Obedience

Stand in the Gap for Your Children

How To Get Your Prayers Answered

Holy Spirit Gifts Series

Number One Way To Fight the Devil

Why You Should Speak In Tongues

Prostitute Faith

You Must Confess Your Faith

What To Do for Healing

God's Medicine of Faith — The Word

How To Triumph Over Sickness

Financial Dominion — How To Take Charge of Your Finances

The Healing Handbook

Rescuing Souls From Hell — Handbook for Effective Soulwinning

How To Cast Out Devils

Power for Living

Radical Christianity

Secrets to Keeping Your Faith Strong

Putting Your Angels To Work

Available from your local bookstore, or by writing:

Harrison House

P. O. Box 35035 • Tulsa, OK 74153

Norvel Hayes shares God's Word boldly and simply, with an enthusiasm that captures the heart of the hearer. He has learned through personal experience that God's Word can be effective in every area of life and that it will work for anyone who will believe it and apply it.

Norvel owns several businesses which function successfully despite the fact that he spends over half his time away from the office, ministering the Gospel throughout the country. His obedience to God and his willingness to share his faith have taken him to a variety of places. He ministers in churches, seminars, conventions, colleges, prisons — anywhere the Spirit of God leads.

For a complete list of tapes and books
by Norvel Hayes, write:
Norvel Hayes
P. O. Box 1379
Cleveland, TN 37311
*Feel free to include your prayer requests and comments
when you write.*